FURNESS A[BBEY]
AND PIEL CA[STLE]

CUMBRIA

❖

Tour by Stuart Harrison
History by Jason Wood
Piel Castle by Rachel Newman

Set in the beautiful Vale of Nightshade are the extensive red sandstone ruins of Furness Abbey, founded by Stephen, later King of England. The abbey first belonged to the Order of Savigny and then to the Cistercians. In its heyday Furness knew prosperity on a huge scale, and, at the time of the Dissolution of the Monasteries in the 1530s, was the second richest Cistercian monastery in England. The importance and wealth of the abbey is reflected in the quality of the upstanding remains. Today the site is one of the most impressive religious monuments in the care of English Heritage.

The first part of this handbook provides a detailed illustrated tour of the site. The second is a history of the abbey from the twelfth century to the present day. The guide concludes with a brief history and description of Piel Castle, once owned by the monks of Furness and now also in the care of English Heritage.

Above: The 'Common seal of the house of the blessed Mary of Furness', as described about its edge. Dating from the 14th century, sprigs of nightshade can be seen behind the shields flanking the Virgin and Child (British Library)

❖ CONTENTS ❖

3 TOUR OF THE ABBEY
3 THE PRECINCT AND OUTER COURT
4 THE CHURCH
5 *The north transept*
6 *The crossing and central tower*
6 *The presbytery and sedilia*
7 *Decoration*
8 *The south transept and traces of the Savigniac church*
8 *The remains of the Savigniac chapter house and the night stairs*
9 *The nave*
10 *The great western tower*
11 THE CLOISTER COURT
11 *The west range*
13 *The south range*
13 *The great frater*
13 *The laver*
13 *The warming house and day stair*
14 *The east range*
I5 *The chapter house*
16 *The parlour and day room*
16 *The dormitory and reredorter*

17 *The infirmary hall*
18 *The infirmary chapel*
18 *The servery and infirmary kitchen*
19 *The first infirmary and abbot's lodging*
20 FEATURES TO THE SOUTH
20 *The misericord*
20 *The visitor centre*
22 HISTORY OF THE ABBEY
22 *Background*
23 *Savigniac origins*
23 *Amalgamation with the Cistercians*
24 *The Furness Abbey crozier*
25 *Growth and prosperity*
27 *Later medieval history*
28 *Monastic economy*
29 *The Dissolution of the Monasteries*
31 *Decline and revival*
32 *The Picturesque and Romantic movements*

37 PIEL CASTLE
38 *Description*

40 FURTHER READING AND ACKNOWLEDGEMENTS

Published by English Heritage, 1 Waterhouse Square, 138-142 Holborn, London EC1 2ST
© English Heritage 1998
First published by English Heritage 1998, reprinted 2003, 2005, 2007, 2009
Revised reprint 2011, 2014
www.english-heritage.org.uk

Photographs by English Heritage Photographic Unit
and copyright English Heritage, unless otherwise stated.

Edited by Louise Wilson. Designed by Pauline Hull.
Printed in England by Pureprint Group
C15, 03/14, 03518, ISBN 978-1-85074-674-4

TOUR OF THE ABBEY

❖

THE PRECINCT AND OUTER COURT

Just as you have passed through the modern entrance of the visitor centre, the medieval visitor had to pass through a strictly controlled system of gates and courts to gain access to the central complex.

The layout of this abbey was slightly different from most other abbey sites as the rising ground on the east and west sides means that the area is constricted. Therefore, instead of being approached from the west in the traditional way, this abbey was built with a main point of entry on the north side.

On entering the site today, the view is of a large lawned area, with the ruins of the church beyond. However in the medieval period this open area was filled with numerous buildings, including a large guest hall, guest houses and their attendant kitchens and stables, now marked by

a range of low walls, the earliest of which date from the twelfth century. These comprise the walls of a porch into a hall which was largely demolished and rebuilt at a higher level in the fourteenth century. The surviving walls of this building were again built over to create a stable, some time after the Dissolution of the Monasteries, and the remains of the walls can still be seen.

In the surviving sill of the porch to the original guesthouse, the

Left: Historiated initial from the cartulary of Furness Abbey of 1412, showing an abbot of Furness with a pope. The cartulary was probably produced at the abbey itself

Below: View of the abbey from the south-east, showing its setting in a narrow wooded valley

The remains of a 12th-century guesthouse beneath those of a later hall

Right: A sephulchral slab that can be seen in the cemetery area

The piscina or washing bowl in the corner of the north chapel of the south transept

remains of a game of Nine Mens' Morris are still visible, carved into the stone. Next to these buildings are the ruins of the wall of the inner court, with the surviving arch of a small gatehouse controlling access between the outer and inner courts. Beyond this gatehouse is the area of the monastic cemetery with several surviving tombs and sepulchral slabs.

Proceed to the doorway of the church ahead of you.

The abbey was originally part of the Order of Savigny, which was absorbed by the Cistercian Order in 1147. We cannot be sure how much of the abbey had by then been completed in stone but it seems fairly certain that the church and buildings surrounding the cloister had been largely finished. These buildings were gradually replaced on a much larger scale during the later twelfth and thirteenth centuries. The remains of the surviving buildings are therefore a complicated mixture of different styles and dates of construction.

THE CHURCH

The church is built on a typical cruciform (cross-shaped) plan. The presbytery (the east end of the church containing the altar) forms the short head of the cross. The north and south transepts, or short arms of the cross, each had three chapels on their east sides and the aisled nave (the long part of the cross) was divided into ten bays. As you can see, the building only partially survives, having lost most of its nave and central tower, though several walls still stand to their full height.

This is the second church to have occupied this site, replacing a slightly smaller, but much more ornate, Savigniac building built in a lavish Romanesque style. When the abbey became Cistercian, the church was gradually rebuilt in the more up-to-date, less ornate, Early Gothic style, though this was done in a piecemeal fashion which left certain parts of the earlier Savigniac building incorporated within its fabric. As the entrance to the site was from the north, the main doorway of the church is in the north transept. It is of elaborate design with an ornate arch and jambs with a mixture of late Romanesque and Early Gothic decoration. This second church was, in turn, considerably remodelled in the fifteenth century, and many of its windows were replaced or enlarged. Above the entrance doorway you can see evidence of one such alteration where several original, round-headed windows have been removed and replaced by a single, very large window which was formerly divided into lights by stone tracery.

*Enter the church by the doorway
leading into the North Transept.*

The north transept

It is in the north transept that the
Early Gothic design of the building
can be best appreciated. The three
great eastern arches, supported on
slender columns formed by groups
of eight round shafts, have delicate
waterleaf capitals, in a French style.
Beyond these were three chapels.
The eastern wall of these has unfortunately been largely demolished, but
part of the altar platforms, with the
bases of the altars can still be seen.
Parts of the flooring and a pillar
piscina (washing bowl) in the corner
of the southern chapel also remain.
The chapels were covered by stone-
ribbed vaulting, though this was
removed and replaced by timber
ceilings sometime in the fifteenth
century, when the east wall was
rebuilt. Above the chapel entrance
arches there is a middle storey, the
triforium, which was pierced by
round-headed arches supported by
shafts. Above each of these arches, in
the top level or clerestory, there was
originally a tall, round-headed
window. Traces of these remain,
though they were later replaced.

Many of the walls of the abbey
have suffered from sinkage due to
insufficient foundations. The north
transept was particularly badly
affected, and, in the 1920s, it had to
be heavily underpinned with concrete

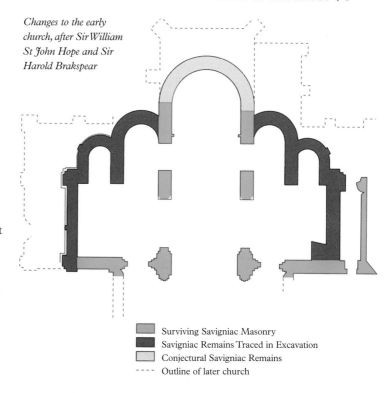

*Changes to the early
church, after Sir William
St John Hope and Sir
Harold Brakspear*

▢ Surviving Savigniac Masonry
▢ Savigniac Remains Traced in Excavation
▢ Conjectural Savigniac Remains
---- Outline of later church

and a ring beam inserted into the wall-
tops. During these repairs it was
discovered that the foundations con-
sisted of oak piles.

The transepts were screened off
where they crossed the nave, and
against the north-west pier there is
the base of a stair which may have
given access to a timber loft on top
of the screen wall. Such lofts were
common in monastic churches and
often held the organ.

*Move to the crossing, or centre, of
the church.*

*Stabilisation work to the
north transept of the abbey
church in the 1920s*

A 'wild man' or 'green man' carving once positioned in the frater, now in the museum

The magnificent sedilia near the high altar

The crossing and central tower

The crossing was the centre of the church, and, extending westwards from it into the first two bays of the nave, were the timber choirstalls in which the monks assembled for their daily round of services. There is now little evidence of these except parts of the lower sections of the base walls which supported the stalls. Above the crossing was the huge central tower, though only the eastern arch which supported it now survives, with a small part of its superstructure above. The heavy tower was carried on four large piers, or pillars, substantial parts of which survive from the Savigniac church. It seems that, in the fifteenth century, the tower must have shown signs of collapse,

and various alterations were made to prevent this, including building a large buttress against the south-west pier, to prop it up. This buttress is covered by panelled tracery and almost conceals the earlier pier.

Walk eastwards into the presbytery.

The presbytery and sedilia

The presbytery was rebuilt twice, first during the Early Gothic remodelling of the church and then later in the fifteenth century, when it was equipped with much larger windows with stone tracery. Despite these two rebuildings, the large blocked round arches which can be seen in the side walls as you enter, survive from the Savigniac presbytery. Some sections of the Early Gothic presbytery also survive above them, including traces of the windows at clerestory level. Flanking the high altar, which stood beneath the east window, were the sedilia, or seats, which were used by the priest and his assistants during the celebration of mass. The Furness sedilia is one of the most impressive in the country. There is a small cupboard and a piscina at the east end. The whole is covered by seven vaulted, tabernacled canopies of intricate design. Near the high altar a notable burial was uncovered during repairs in 2010 (see page 24).

Retrace your steps to the crossing and turn left into the south transept

❖ DECORATION ❖

Many of the alterations to the church which can be easily recognised today, such as enlarged windows, would have been largely disguised in medieval times because the whole church was limewashed internally and externally. If you look carefully you can still see a white coating on some of the abbey stonework. The limewash was usually covered with a decorative false masonry pattern in red, white or black paint with stippled flower motifs and chevron patterns. The piers and arches may have been painted with large striped bandings or sometimes vine trails. Towards the end of the abbey's life, the backs of the altars were often equipped with elaborate reredos panels which featured figurative sculptures made from alabaster, brightly painted and gilded. The later church would therefore have looked very colourful while the earlier church, when originally built, was more austere with the use of decoration, sculpture and statues largely forbidden.

A reconstruction drawing by Peter Urmstone of the choir of the medieval church at St Augustine's Abbey, Canterbury. Although different to the church at Furness Abbey, it shows the colourful decoration used in abbey churches Below: A tomb base still to be seen in the church nave. Drawing from Annales Furnesienses by T Beck

A column niche in the south transept

Opposite: Early photograph of the night stairs in the south transept by Roger Fenton in 1856

A band of decorative mouldings from the early Savigniac church, re-used as facing stones in one of the south transept chapels

The south transept and traces of the Savigniac church

The south transept is very similar to the north but the chapels on its east side were more substantially remodelled in the fifteenth century. The northernmost chapel was extended eastwards and the additional space used as a sacristy for the storage of plate and vestments used during the services. As in the north transept, the vaulting in these chapels was removed and replaced by timber ceilings supported on stone corbels. On the eastern side, or back, of the arcade (best seen from within the chapels) just above the arches, is a band of decorative Romanesque mouldings salvaged from the Savigniac church and reused as facing stones. It is interesting to note that, as twentieth-century visitors, we are seeing something that would have been invisible in medieval times, because it would

have been above the level of the low, wooden ceiling. Much of the walling above these mouldings is also reused material. The transepts of the Savigniac church were smaller than their replacements and featured two chapels on the eastern side which terminated in apsidal or rounded east walls. Careful measurement of the reused pieces of stone shows that they formed parts of the arches at the entrances to the chapels and sections of their curved apsidal east walls.

The remains of the Savigniac chapter house and the night stairs

When the transepts were rebuilt they were extended and the south transept butted up to the north wall of the chapter house. Interesting evidence for this is a hole in the facing of the south wall of the south chapel, in which the apsidal or round east wall of this chapter house has been uncovered, with the jamb of one of its windows. In the middle of the south wall are a pair of projecting corbel brackets which it is thought supported a clock. Next to these, further to the west, there is a doorway set high above the floor of the church, and formerly approached by a stone staircase, which was used by the monks as their entrance for the night services.

Return to the crossing and turn left into the nave.

The nave

The original impressive height of the
nave can still be seen from the walls
standing at its west end. Though it is
now largely ruined to a low level, parts
of the first arch of the arcade on the
south side survive. This arch was
blocked up to help stabilise the
collapsing central tower. Behind this,
the south aisle wall stands relatively
intact with a single pointed, or lancet,
window and the outline of the stone
vaulting which covered the aisle is
still visible. The pointed form of the
aisle window stands in marked con-
trast to the round-headed designs
used in the transepts, and indicates
to archaeologists that there may have
been a delay in rebuilding the nave
of the Savigniac church after the
reconstruction of the presbytery and
transepts. Other recent evidence
confirms that this was the case and
that the nave was rebuilt to a largely
old-fashioned, conservative design to
harmonise with the transepts. The
positions of the rest of the missing
arcades are marked by the stumps
of the large piers which had an alter-
nating arrangement of eight shafted
designs, like those in the transepts,
and plain simple cylinders of large
diameter, parts of which may have
been salvaged from the Savigniac
nave arcades.

The division of the nave

The nave was divided by two screens
into three distinct spaces. At the

ROYAL PHOTOGRAPHIC SOCIETY, BATH

Above: Huby's Tower at Fountains Abbey. Below: The remains of the columns in the nave at Furness and the great west tower

eastern end of the nave there was the monks' choir, with the first screen, known as the pulpitum screen, on its western side. There was then a space, known as the retrochoir, with the second screen, the rood screen, on its west side. Beyond the rood screen most of the nave was occupied by the choir of the lay brothers. To accommodate this western choir, solid walls were added to the aisles to screen them off from the nave. These were set along, and bonded to, the fronts of the piers.

The lay brothers also attended night services and you can see the doorway from their dormitory, and traces of the staircase leading from it into the church, at the west end of the south aisle. When the lay brothers had ceased to form a part of the community, their stalls were removed, together with the flanking screen walls, and the fronts of the piers were remodelled. The nave then became an open space used for processions. The pulpitum and rood screens were renewed in stone with elaborate niches and canopies, though only the lowest of these now survive. As the aisles were no longer required as passageways, they too were partially divided up into separate chapel spaces. The remains of some of these can be seen in the north aisle.

The great western tower

In the late fifteenth century there was a general trend towards tower building. At abbeys such as Furness, where the central tower could not be enlarged for structural reasons, a completely new tower was added to some other part of the church. Here, a huge new tower with a large traceried west window was constructed at the west end of the church. Externally, it has deeply projecting buttresses with elaborate canopied niches and pedestals for statues. Though now reduced to a height of around sixty feet, the remains are

very similar to Huby's tower at Fountains Abbey, which is 160 feet high. There can be little doubt that the Furness tower also rose to a similar height. To accommodate the magnificent new tower, the west front of the church and first bay of the nave arcades were demolished and a revised western entrance contrived at the end of the north aisle. Because of the changes in ground level, this was approached by an internal staircase.

From the west end of the nave go through the doorway in the south aisle into the cloister court.

THE CLOISTER COURT

It is difficult to get a feel today for what the cloister area must have been like, as it was once surrounded by high buildings, creating a rectangular court that would have felt quite enclosed. When complete, it had covered alleys on each side supported on elegant open arcading. This was rebuilt several times and by the thirteenth century had trefoiled arches standing on pairs of marble bases, shafts and capitals, some of which are displayed in the visitor centre. The successive marks of the different roofs of these covered alleys can be seen on the surviving walls of the nave and east range. It was here that the monks spent much of their time studying and writing at carrels, or

desks, in the northern alley. The central garth was often laid out as a formal garden with paths and raised beds. The Savigniac cloister and monastic buildings were smaller than the present layout, which was extended southwards as the Cistercians progressively rebuilt the monastery.

View of the cloister from the west tower

The west range

The first monastic building to be rebuilt was the range on the western side of the cloister which now survives as a series of low walls. The surviving details, such as the central row of pier bases, show that, like the transepts, the west range was of Early Gothic design. It had two floors and the ground floor was divided into fifteen double bays, covered with stone groined vaults and divided at intervals into separate rooms. At the north end, there was an outer parlour

The remains of the west range of the cloister as it appears today

two bays long, then four bays for storage. The main cloister entrance, or parlour, took up the next bay, with the rest of the range to the south forming the lay brothers' frater, or dining hall. Above these rooms, the whole of the first floor formed the lay brothers' dormitory with a stair at the northern end (already seen from within the church) for the monks to attend night services. On the west side was a series of smaller buildings and covered alleys, with a detached reredorter, or latrine building to the south-west. This was reached from the lay brothers' dormitory by a bridge. Little now survives except the ashlar-faced drain channel which took away the waste. When the lay brothers had ceased to be part of the community the west range was subdivided into several smaller rooms with fireplaces for greater comfort.

Reconstruction drawing of the great frater at Rievaulx Abbey by Alan Sorrell

The south range

Between the west and east ranges are a series of low walls, some of which can still be seen in the grass, indicating the site of the southern range of buildings. The Savigniac frater, or refectory, was originally built parallel to the south alley of the cloister, and there is evidence for its progressive enlargement. Finally, in the thirteenth century, the whole range was rebuilt further south on a massively enlarged scale. There must have been frequent building work in progress to disturb the monks!

The great frater

The new frater projected at a right angle south of the cloister alley. Measuring around 150 feet long by nearly forty feet wide, it was one of the largest ever built by the Cistercians. A few surviving fragments show that, like the better surviving examples at Fountains and Rievaulx, it had elaborate wall arcades, a pulpit in the west wall supported on a marble corbel and a cornice carved with grotesque heads (now displayed in the visitor centre). The monks sat on raised benches set around the side walls at tables supported by fixed stone legs. They ate in silence except for one, who would stand in the pulpit and read a passage from scrip-

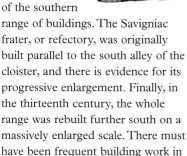

ture or a good book. The meals were simple and vegetarian, as the Rule of St Benedict forbade the eating of flesh meats. By the fourteenth century, the monks had obtained dispensation from the Pope to eat meat on certain days, though it had to be cooked in a separate kitchen and eaten in a separate frater known as the misericord, which you will see later.

The laver

Flanking the frater doorway in the south alley of the cloister would have been a series of long troughs, known as the laver, with a piped water supply, so that the monks might wash before and after meals. It was here that the monks performed the Mandatum on Saturdays and Maundy Thursday, washing the feet of the brethren as Christ washed the feet of the Disciples before the Last Supper.

The warming house and day stair

Between the frater and the east range was the warming house where a fire was kept burning from All Saints Day until Good Friday, so that the monks might keep warm in the winter months.

A capital from the frater decorated with carvings of apes (now displayed in the visitor centre). Drawing by Judith Dobie

The east range of the abbey buildings

There was a day stair leading from here to the dormitory, the outline of which can still be seen against the wall of the east range, with the doorway to the dormitory at the top.

Walk back up the east cloister alley towards the church.

The five elaborate arches in the east range of the abbey

The east range

The east range of the cloister formed the principal living quarters of the choir monks. The exceptionally large size of this range suggests that there were a large number of monks when it was built. There are a series of very fine, large and elaborately moulded round-headed arches of thirteenth-century date. The three arches at the north end form a pair of large book cupboards, with the entrance to the chapter house in the centre. Unfortunately, the soft stonework is badly eroded, but faint traces of the white limewash and red painted lines can be seen on some of the arch stones. The jambs have lost their marble shafts, but the grey marble abaci on top of the capitals still survive. The book cupboards would have housed the abbey library and the faint remains of the sockets and fittings for the book shelves are still visible on the walls. The chapter house doorway gives entrance to a vaulted vestibule with an elaborately carved vault boss at its centre and trefoiled arches, with marble bases and capitals, along the side walls. Beyond is the great chapter house.

Enter the chapter house through the fourth archway

The chapter house

This chapter house replaced a more modest Savigniac building. The new chapter house was resplendent with large windows and a ribbed vault carried on tall moulded piers. A considerable amount of marble was used for the wall shafts and other details. It was darkly polished and would have contrasted starkly with the white painted walls. It was in this room that the monks met daily to confess faults, receive punishment and hear a chapter read from the Rule of St Benedict (hence the name chapter house).

Business matters and policy were also discussed here. The monastery was a powerful and influential organisation, and the Abbot and his senior monks met here in the same way that a board of company directors would meet today.

The abbot sat at the centre of the east wall, with the monks, in order of seniority, on benches ranged round the walls. The central space would have been taken up with the tomb slabs of earlier abbots and, though none now survive *in situ*, a few are displayed in the visitor centre. Above the chapter house there is a second range of windows belonging to a

Mid 19th-century artist's reconstruction of the chapter house vestibule

The interior of the chapter house

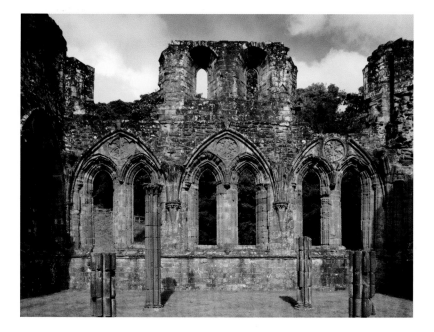

The east range and main watercourse

An elaborate stiff-leaved corbel at the north end of the day-room

through the range and a long room divided by a central row of columns into thirteen vaulted double bays. This was the day room, and a series of now blocked arches in the south and east walls are thought to suggest that it was in part used for the pursuit of manual trades by the monks. Similar arches are known to have had this use at other abbeys and there is no other obvious reason for such large openings unless large pieces of machinery or materials needed to be brought in and out. Later, the Rule of St Benedict was relaxed somewhat and fireplaces and partitions were introduced for more comfort.

The dormitory and reredorter

The whole of the first floor of the east range was taken up with the monks' dormitory, which was connected to the church by a passage over the chapter house vestibule. The dormitory was lit by a series of lancet windows and, though probably originally an open room with the monks sleeping on mattresses, it was later partitioned into separate cubicles. On its east side there was a detached reredorter or latrine, built parallel to the east range and opening straight into the main watercourse underneath. It was approached from the dormitory by a bridge. Its lower walls and the drain channel can still be seen. Like the chapter house, the east wall of the range leans considerably, and was

room that was probably used as an extension to the monks' dormitory. It may have served originally as the abbot's or prior's lodging. The outer walls began to lean so much that, in the 1920s, the chapter house was on the verge of collapse and required extensive underpinning with concrete to save it.

Turn left (south) out of the chapter house

The parlour and day room

You will see that there are two more large doorways. The first leads to a narrow room which was used as the parlour. This was the only part of the cloister where the monks were allowed to speak. The second doorway gives access to a passage propped up with large buttresses to prevent its collapse.

Proceed to the south end of the day room and exit through the gap in the south wall.

The infirmary hall

South of the main cloister ranges is the site of the great infirmary hall built in the late thirteenth century. The infirmary complex was provided for those monks too sick or infirm to take part in the normal monastic routine, and the surviving remains show that this was one of the largest such halls built by the Cistercians. Permanently ill or infirm monks lived here all the time, and the buildings therefore duplicate many of the rooms of the main abbey, such as the kitchen, chapel and latrines. The main part of this large building has been reduced to a low level but the eastern part, which includes the chapel, survives largely intact. The great hall, which extended westwards from the surviving block, was one hundred and twenty five feet long by nearly fifty feet wide and appears to have been roofed with a single span. It may have been a surprisingly early and remarkable example of hammer-beam design.

The jamb of one of the large traceried windows in this room can be seen at the east end of the north wall. At the west end was a separate pantry with cupboards in its west wall. The remains of the east wall, against the chapel block, with its two tiers of

The reredorter or latrine channel behind the monks' dormitory

The infirmary chapel, servery and kitchen from above the abbot's lodging

blind arcades, give an impression of what has been lost. The great hall would have been divided up by timber screens into a series of cubicles, with beds for the residents. In some of the wall recesses were fireplaces. The main entrance was in the second bay from the east on the north side and was approached by a covered pentice from the warming house.

Enter the chapel on the south of this building.

A grotesque human head from a cornice

The infirmary chapel

The chapel is a large room covered with three bays of fine ribbed vaulting. The great east window was of unusual design in which the arched head followed the curvature of the internal vaulting. It was filled with a series of circular panels with cusped subdivisions. Much survives of the wall bench running all round the room, and in the south wall at the east end is the remains of an elaborate piscina, used for cleaning the altar vessels after the mass. The three windows in the south wall also mirror the shape of the vaulting and this gives an unusual triangular shape to the arch heads. Here the window tracery is better preserved, with cusped circles in the arches.

Leave the chapel and enter the adjoining room on the north side.

A medieval cresset lamp on display in the museum at the abbey. It consists of five cups hollowed out of sandstone, with wicks floating in oil – a common form of lighting in the middle ages

The servery and infirmary kitchen

This room formed an antechamber and servery to the great hall with paired doorways in the west wall. It is covered by two bays of ribbed vaults with a doorway at the north-east corner to a spiral staircase which gave access to the upper chambers, for the infirmarer, above the chapel. Centrally placed in the north wall is another doorway which gave access through an angled passage to the great kitchen. Set low on one of the external buttresses is a corbel carved in the form of a grotesque head.

The kitchen was a detached building standing to the north-east of the infirmary block and was of irregular polygonal plan with eight sides. Now reduced to low walls, it is difficult to appreciate how it would have appeared when complete. In two of its angles there are traces of fireplaces with a stone trough and a rubbish chute into the main watercourse which runs beneath the building. It was probably completed with a stone rib-vaulted roof as a fire precaution. No doubt there were more fireplaces than the two which have survived and possibly a central hearth which helped support the vaults.

Cross the watercourse to the building on the east side.

The first infirmary and abbot's lodging

The ruins of this substantial building are complex and have been identified as the earlier infirmary and subsequent abbot's lodging. Originally it comprised a single rectangular block, rib-vaulted on the ground floor, with a central row of four columns. Each bay was lit by paired lancet windows, except the central bay of the east wall which had a large fireplace with a fireplace hood supported on large corbels. Next to the main entrance in the south wall is an unusual trefoil-shaped squint with a similar one (now blocked) opposite it in the north wall.

The building was enlarged when a latrine block was added on the north end with a drain branching from the main watercourse. This was controlled by a series of paddle sluices and the sockets for these have survived. The building was substantially extended by cutting into the adjoining cliff on its east side and spanning arches between the existing building and the cliff face to support extra rooms above. These were reached by a spiral staircase near the north end of the east wall and, at its most extensive, the building must have been substantially larger on its upper floors than the surviving ground floor would initially indicate. This extension overloaded the original structure and its vaults began to spread the side walls. To prevent this threatened collapse, three large flying buttresses were constructed against the west wall, though only the lower parts of these now survive. As the abbot's lodging, it would have been provided with a suite of rooms such as a hall, dining chamber, bedroom, secretariat and private chapel. Parts of the upper floors still survive today.

An archbishop and six bishops, from the cartulary of Furness Abbey, 1412

The seal of the abbots of Furness, dating from the 13th century

The ruins of the abbot's lodgings at the abbey

The medieval Bow Bridge near the abbey site

FEATURES TO THE SOUTH

To the south-east, outside the fenced enclosure and across the road, there is a small cottage, which, for many years, served as the residence of the abbey custodian. Remarkably, this building retained its medieval roof relatively intact until 1996 when it was burnt out by vandals. It was the only abbey building to have remained roofed since the Dissolution of the Monasteries.

Further east, along the road, there survives the medieval Bow Bridge. The area to the south of the abbey is known as the Amphitheatre because of its bowl shape. It retains a number of earthwork features, including traces of the abbey quarries and depressions thought to have been formerly the abbey fishponds. Along the crest of the hill is a substantial stretch of the medieval precinct wall.

Return along the eastern side of the ruins towards the church.

The misericord

Near the south end of the eastern range are the low walls of a square building, with fifteenth-century diagonal corner buttresses which straddled the main watercourse. Its proximity to the infirmary kitchen suggests that it was the misericord (the refectory where red meat could be eaten). The ground floor was divided into two rooms and evidently had an upper floor, accessed by a staircase in its north-west corner. This may have connected with the dormitory by a bridge. Along its north side was a pentice, or covered alley, which allowed access from the undercroft of the east range to the abbot's lodging.

There are splendid views as you walk back along the east side of the ruins towards the visitor centre.

The wooden shed just inside the northern perimeter fence was the custodian's hut in Victorian times. Though small, it has its own fireplace and chimney.

The visitor centre

The visitor centre houses an education centre and an extensive exhibition about the history of the abbey. The highlight of the exhibition is undoubtedly the crozier and ring from the burial discovered in the presbytery in 2012. The remarkable crozier and ring discovered in a burial in the presbytery (see page 24) are displayed, as is also a fascinating collection of pillars and pieces of stone from the abbey which have been conserved and placed here for protection.

As you leave the main abbey site through the visitor centre, you will see the remains of the great gatehouse straddling the road. This was the main point of access into the walled monastic precinct. It was placed within the precinct and approached down a walled lane from a smaller outer gate in the precinct wall. The great gatehouse had a gate passage, probably vaulted, with an internal cross-partition formed by a large carriage arch and a smaller pedestrian arch. It was on these two arches that the gates were hung. To the north, the position of the outer gate is now marked by the rebuilt arch spanning the road.

Access to the site today is therefore very close to what it was when the abbey was complete.

Adjoining the outer gate are the almost complete remains of the capella, or gatehouse chapel with traces of its altar and fine arched sedilia in the south wall.

Engravings of effigies from the church nave, now in the visitor centre. The knights are unusual for their closed visors. Published in T Beck's Annales Furnesienses

HISTORY OF THE ABBEY

Self-portrait of John Stell, monk of Furness Abbey, showing himself as a scribe, with pen and knife; from the cartulary of Furness, 1412

Background

The abbey of St Mary of Furness lies in a secluded, steep-sided valley situated in the southern part of the Furness peninsula. Formerly part of Lancashire, the area's situation between the waters of Morecambe Bay, the undrained lands of South Cumbria and the inhospitable hills of Lakeland was one of singular isolation.

However, the location was well chosen, as the valley provided a sheltered site for the abbey precinct, a ready supply of water, and access to abundant timber and stone for building. Roads to the north through the nearby town of Dalton, and low-tide tracks to the east across the estuaries of the rivers Kent and Leven, provided a means of inland communication. The haven enclosed by Walney Island provided access by sea and communications with the Isle of Man and Ireland.

The history of Furness Abbey is in many ways an exceptional one. From being a subordinate member of the minor congregation of Savigny, it rose to become a powerful and important religious house and, at the time of its suppression, was the second richest Cistercian monastery in England, after Fountains Abbey in Yorkshire. For over 400 years, the abbey enjoyed substantial privileges, possessions and wealth, and had a major influence on both regional and national affairs. Unfortunately, our knowledge of the medieval history of Furness is sketchy because many of the contemporary records were lost after the Dissolution of the Monasteries in the late 1530s.

For the post-medieval period the historical sources are rich. This is hardly surprising in view of the fact that the abbey has spent more than half of its life as a ruin. As such it has been a focus for antiquarian study, romantic excursion and, later, popular tourism. Its interest for modern visitors and archaeologists is now in all these aspects of its history.

Savigniac origins

Furness Abbey was the first and most important foundation of the Savigniac Order in the British Isles. This newly-established congregation had started in northern France at Savigny in Mortain. In 1124, a group of Savigniac monks was invited by Stephen, then Count of Boulogne and Mortain and later King of England, to settle at Tulketh (near Preston) in Lancashire. We know the name of the first leader or abbot, Ewan d'Avranches, a former monk of Savigny, but virtually nothing else is known of this initial foundation. After only three years Tulketh was abandoned and the community relocated to the valley of Bekansgill in Furness where the abbey was founded.

In the twenty-year period between the foundation of Furness Abbey and the amalgamation of the Savigniac order with that of the Cistercians, twelve more Savigniac houses were established in England and Wales, as well as one in the Isle of Man and two in Ireland.

Amalgamation with the Cistercians

In 1147, the entire congregation of Savigny was incorporated into the much larger and more powerful Cistercian Order. This merger, instigated by Abbot Serlo of Savigny, was opposed by the abbot of Furness, Peter of York. However, after some resistance, Furness eventually accepted Cistercian rule in about 1150. Peter resigned and was replaced by a new abbot from Savigny itself. Furness thus became a Cistercian monastery and part of an international order of formidable strength.

The Cistercians, or 'White Monks' as they were known, because of the undyed habits they wore, had a reputation for austerity and seclusion from secular life. Much of their time was spent performing routine daily services, or in private prayer, reading and study. Although some physical work was undertaken by these so-called choir monks, most tasks that required heavy manual labour were delegated to conversi or lay brothers. These were men from a poor background who were usually illiterate. Lay brothers lived similar but separate lives from the choir monks, taking simpler religious vows and attending fewer church services. The lay brothers acted as a kind of buffer between the choir monks and the outside world. In later years, the more prominent among them played key roles in the commercial and business affairs of the monastery.

Engraving of a statue of King Stephen, from Annales Furnesienses *by T Beck*

Lay brother reaping corn

❖ THE FURNESS ABBEY CROZIER ❖

During emergency repairs to the presbytery in 2010, archaeologists uncovered several burials. One proved spectacular – the first high status burial of its kind to be excavated in this country in almost 50 years and one affording a unique opportunity to understand more about Cistercian burial practice and the community at Furness. Within the presbytery, near the site of the high altar were the remains of a man between 40 and 50 years old. He was buried some time after the end of the 13th century, and before the dissolution of the monastery in 1537. A crozier was laid over his left shoulder, its shaft of ash wood (originally painted) extended to his feet and ended in a spiked iron tip. The head of the crozier, of gilded copper alloy, may have been made in the 12th century as a simple hook ending in the head of a serpent. Later, probably before the end of the 14th century, identical decorated discs of gilded silver were fitted over each side of the crook. They depict St Michael the Archangel wrestling with a dragon.

A fragment of linen and silk fabric, part of the sweat cloth (the sudarium) that was attached to the staff below the crozier head and hung down the sides of the crook, was found preserved inside the knop of the crozier.

On the man's right hand was a gilded silver ring set with a white stone (possibly rock crystal or white sapphire). The underside of the ring mount ends in a point, possibly intended to mortify the flesh. This underside is hollow, and may have contained a fragment of a holy relic.

From the 13th century onwards most Cistercian abbots were buried in the chapter house (see page 15). When this was full they may have been buried in the church, but the presbytery was reserved for patrons rich enough to secure a burial place in this most prestigious part of the church. It is not known who the man buried here was, though he must have been of very high status – he may have been an abbot, either rich enough or highly regarded enough to be buried here, or he may have been one of the two bishops of Man known to have been buried at Furness Abbey.

Above and left: The ring found on the right hand of a man buried within the presbytery, and the crozier that was laid over his left shoulder

Growth and prosperity

As the number of monks at Furness increased, several new monasteries were colonised from the abbey. Three of these 'daughter houses' date from the early years of the Savigniac occupation. Calder Abbey in Cumbria and Rushen Abbey on the Isle of Man were both founded in 1134, and Swineshead Abbey in Lincolnshire in 1135. Unfortunately, a Scottish raid in 1137 caused Calder to be abandoned. The monks were forced to return to Furness, where they were refused entry and had to relocate to Yorkshire. The furness monks were probably unwilling to take in more mouths to feed! The site at Calder was later refounded in 1142. Under the Cistercians two further daughter houses were established in Ireland, at Inch in 1180 and Abington in 1205.

A land endowment by Stephen meant that the abbey quickly became the predominant landowner in Low Furness and the Furness Fells. Further acquisitions in the thirteenth century included estates in Borrowdale and upper Eskdale, and large ranges in the Pennines at the head of Ribblesdale and on the flanks of Ingleborough and Whernside.

The church at Calder Abbey, an early Savigniac daughter house of Furness Abbey

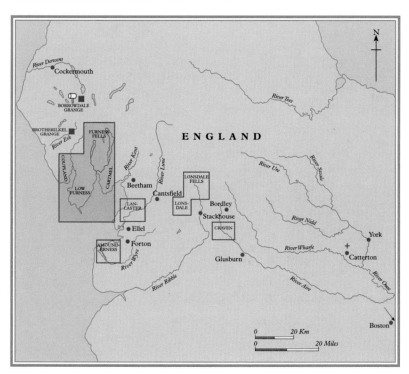

*Left: Furness Abbey's land-holdings in the north of England. (It also owned land in the Isle of Man, and Ireland). *For a more detailed map of the abbey's lands in the Furness area see page 26*

From its geographically isolated position, the abbey dominated its region and achieved a degree of independence rare among monasteries. At Furness, the abbot enjoyed the powers and privileges of a feudal lord and border baron. He also had the right to nominate the bishop of the Isle of Man. This autonomous position was further consolidated in later years as the abbot's military, political and administrative responsibilities grew.

Location of Furness Abbey's possessions in the region of Low Furness and the Furness Fells

- ★ Furness Abbey
- ▣ Granges
- • Other properties
- ⊕ Appropriated churches
- + Chapels
- Cornmill
- Fulling mill
- Tanning
- Rabbit warren
- Seafowl & eggs
- Quarry
- Millstones
- Iron mines
- Forges
- Castles
- P Peat
- S Salt pans
- Fishing
- Oyster beds

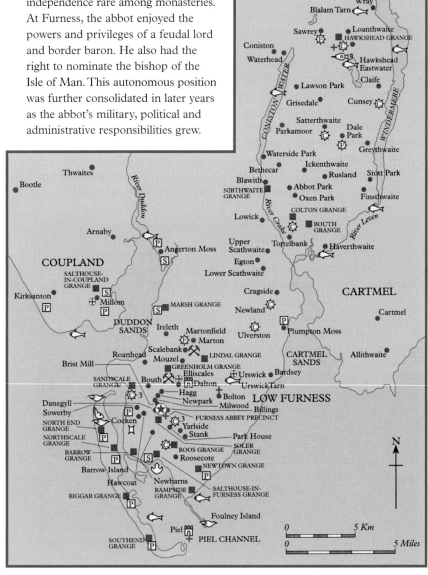

FURNESS COUCHER BOOK/BRITISH LIBRARY

Later medieval history

The location of Furness Abbey made it vulnerable to raids from Scotland. In the early fourteenth century, border warfare flared up again following the defeat of the English at Bannockburn. The Furness peninsula was attacked in 1316 and six years later Robert Bruce headed another raid. This time, however, as the Lanercost Chronicle notes, the abbot of Furness, John Cockerham, entertained Robert Bruce at the abbey, '. . . and paid ransom for the district of Furness that it should not again be burnt or plundered.' Following the Scottish raids, the small fort protecting the Walney haven, on what became known as Piel Island, was re-garrisoned and substantially rebuilt as a castle from 1327. (For a history and description of Piel Castle see page 38).

At about this time, two exceptional privileges were added to the abbot's powers. These were the right to act in place of the sheriff and the right to appoint his own coroner. During this period, the abbot's principal courts were established at Dalton.

A series of crises in the fourteenth century, including famine, plague and war with France, badly affected the Cistercian economy. Against this background, it is not surprising that Furness found itself in financial difficulties. Faced with these problems the abbey began to abandon direct involvement in agriculture. Much of its land was leased and the monks relied largely on rents for income. By the end of the century, the number of lay brothers had greatly diminished, as the need for an effective labour force was reduced.

During the fifteenth century, the number of monks in residence at the abbey also grew smaller. A relaxation of the Cistercian rule now permitted laymen to live on the site on the same terms as lay brothers had done before. These laymen sometimes included state pensioners billeted upon the abbey by the King.

The last forty years of the abbey's existence were marked by a general decline in the standing of the monastery and in the abbot's authority. For most of this period the abbot was one Alexander Banke, though a rival, John Dalton, did succeed for a short time in deposing him and taking his place.

Frequent disputes with neighbours and tenants had the Church on the defensive. One of the most celebrated disputes occurred in 1516.

A monk of Furness Abbey, probably meant to represent Robert Denton, abbot in the 1230s; from the cartulary of Furness, 1412

Two lay brothers chopping down a tree, from an illuminated manuscript

BRITISH LIBRARY

❖ MONASTIC ECONOMY ❖

Furness Abbey was, among other things, a centre of a business enterprise controlling a large and well-organised estate spread over a wide area, including parts of Ireland. The estate was organised into compact blocks of land and managed from large farms or granges. These were operated by hired labour and by the lay brothers from the abbey. Furness possessed a great number of granges.

Lay brothers chopping wood

was no exception. The abbey owned extensive livestock ranches in the marginal lands of the northern fells and the Pennines, from where wool was exported across the North Sea to the weaving towns of Flanders. For the domestic market, fulling mills and tanneries were established for preparing wool and cattle hides.

Natural resources, of which iron ore and charcoal for fuel were the most important,

were valuable assets. The abbey acquired mineral rights over a large area north of Dalton, where it controlled a number of iron mines.

On coastal lands, peat and salt were exploited. The abbey's main cornlands were on Walney Island, and watermills controlled by the abbey were used for grinding the grain. Fish was important in the monastic diet. The abbey had fishing rights throughout the region and a major fishery at Beaumont near Lancaster. The abbey's natural haven, enclosed by Walney Island, was the centre for Manx and Irish seaborne trade in iron, salt, corn and malt.

Remains of a 15th-century grange at Hawkshead

The success of the Cistercian economy was based in part on the ability of the abbeys to farm previously uncultivated lands in a profitable way and to develop sheep farming and from it a trade in wool. Furness

A water mill from the Luttrell Psalter

The signatures of the abbot, prior and monks of Furness on the deed surrendering the abbey to the king, 9 April 1537

Abbot Banke was taken to court by William Case and his wife Isobel on behalf of the people of Sellergarth, a small farming hamlet near the abbey. It was charged that '. . . the said Abbot with more than 22 of his monks . . . in riotous manner . . . turned out the said plaintiffs . . . to the plaintiffs' utter undoing.' The abbot had razed the hamlet and turned it into arable land for sheep

The Dissolution of the Monasteries

Early in 1536, Parliament passed an Act for suppressing the smaller monasteries. This was one of a series of Henry VIII's measures to bring the Church under state control. When the protest against the suppression, known as the Pilgrimage of Grace, broke out, the monks of Furness were implicated. The last abbot, Roger Pyle, seems to have capitulated. Rather than face trial for treason he offered to give up the abbey and its possessions to the King. Furness was thus the first of the major monasteries to be dissolved. The deed of surrender was signed by the abbot, the prior (the abbot's deputy) and twenty-eight monks on 9 April 1537.

On 23 June 1537, Robert Southwell, the Court's Receiver, arrived with three other Commissioners to survey Furness Abbey and dispose of its estate. It is clear from a letter of 3 July, written by Southwell to Thomas Cromwell, the King's chief minister, that the lead was being stripped from the roofs, the tracery of the windows broken, and the buildings dismantled even while the monks were still in residence.

Sir John Lamplieu, the high sheriff of Cumberland, was placed in charge of the site and lands and took up residence at Furness early in 1538. Accordingly, some of the abbey

One of the earliest known views of Furness Abbey: an engraving of 1727 from the east by Samuel and Nathaniel Buck

buildings, probably including the former abbot's house, were left in a habitable state for his domestic and agricultural purposes.

In 1540 the site was leased to Sir Thomas Curwen and passed to his son-in-law, John Preston, in 1546. A document from the Lancashire Pleadings in the Duchy Court, dated February 1549, alludes to the ruinous state of the 'Halle and other Howses' and the desire of Preston to erect a 'newe Halle parler Chambres and other howses of offices'. Unfortunately, the document does not make it clear where these new buildings were to be, and we

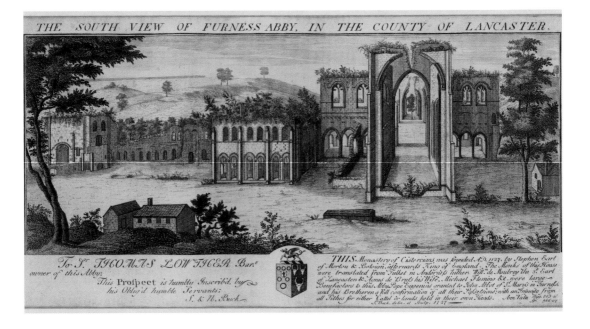

Part of another engraving of 1727 showing a manor house to the north of the abbey ruins

don't know whether Preston ever built them. However, construction of a manor house and associated buildings is known to have taken place by about 1671, when Sir Daniel Fleming noted the presence of 'a stately new house'.

Decline and revival

The site of the abbey remained in the Preston family for several generations. It then passed by marriage to the Lowthers (who preferred to live at Holker Hall) and finally to the Cavendishes. From the late seventeenth century, the manor house was occupied by a variety of tenants. By the second half of the eighteenth century, the building was in decline, having been leased out for agricultural and other purposes. An estate map drawn for Lord George Cavendish by William Gibson in 1775 shows that by this date the manor had degenerated into a mere farmhouse.

However, during the 1780s, some refurbishment of a part of the building was undertaken, to allow the Cavendish family the occasional visit to the site.

From the early nineteenth century a visit to the ruins was considered an essential part of any trip to the Lake District. William Wordsworth's Guide to the Lakes did much to make the abbey a popular tourist attraction.

Extract from an estate map by William Gibson from a manuscript dated 1775 in the private collections at Holker Hall

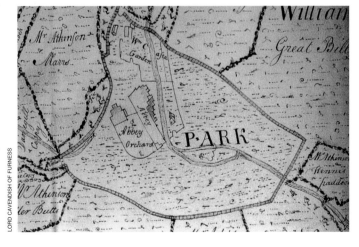

❖ THE PICTURESQUE ANI

During the late eighteenth and early nineteenth centuries, there was a growing appreciation of the picturesque and romantic qualities of ruins as landscape features and as historic monuments. A number of important drawings, prints, topographical studies and descriptions of Furness Abbey belong to this period.

Of particular interest is the earliest known plan of the abbey by Thomas West, drawn in about 1770 and first published in his *Antiquities of Furness* in 1774. The plan was accompanied by a two-page explanatory key and list of dimensions. William Gilpin's description of 1772 and accompanying aquatint of the infirmary chapel were published in his *Observations relative chiefly to Picturesque Beauty ...* in 1786. Gilpin wrote that the abbey '...has suffered, from the hand of time, only such depredations as picturesque beauty requires.'

Two drawings of the church made in 1777 by Thomas Hearne were later published as engravings in 1786 by Hearne and William Byrne in their *Antiquities of Great Britain*. An early watercolour of the church crossing by Edward Dayes dates to 1795, while a pencil sketch of the same view, together with others of the infirmary

Aquatint of the infirmary chapel by John Smith published by William Gilpin in 1786

chapel and outer gate, were made by the young J M W Turner in 1797.

A Journey made in the summer of 1794, published by the Gothic novelist Ann (Mrs) Radcliffe in 1795, epitomises the late eighteenth-century picturesque view of the site:

'*... the character of the deserted ruin is scrupulously preserved in the surrounding area; no spade has dared to level the inequalities which fallen fragments have occasioned in the ground, or shears to clip the wild fern and underwood that overspread it; but every circumstance conspires to heighten the solitary grace of the principal object, and to prolong the luxurious melancholy which the view of it inspires.*'

Several important pictorial references belong to the early nineteenth century. Two drawings of the church and infirmary chapel by William Green in 1804 were later published in his *Tourist's New Guide* in 1819. Two engravings of the church and east range by William Close were published in 1805 as additional illustrations in Close's revised edition of *West's Antiquities of Furness*. Various drawings and watercolours by John Buckler and his son date to 1814, while Theodore

ROMANTIC MOVEMENTS ❖

Fielding's aquatint of the church was published by Fielding and J Walton in 1821 in their *Picturesque Tour of the English Lakes* (see back cover)

A very interesting depiction of the site is an engraving of the church published by Joseph Wilkinson in 1810 in his *Select Views in Cumberland, Westmorland and Lancashire*. William Wordsworth's *Guide to the Lakes* was first published as an anonymous introduction to Wilkinson's volume. The poet, who as a young man had a close affinity with the abbey, was highly critical of Wilkinson's artistic abilities. In a letter to Lady Beaumont he wrote: *'The drawings, or etchings, or whatever they may be called, are … intolerable. You will receive from them that sort of disgust which I do from bad poetry … They will please many who in all the arts are most taken with what is worthless.'*

Right: A view of the church drawn by Joseph Wilkinson, engraved by WF Wells, and published by Wilkinson in 1810

From Wordsworth's *The Prelude*, published in 1805:

> … a mouldering Pile, with fractured arch,
> belfry, and images, and living trees,
> A holy scene! along the smooth green turf
> Our horses grazed: to more than inland peace
> Left by the sea wind passing overhead
> (Though wind of roughest temper) trees and towers
> May in that valley oftentimes be seen,
> Both silent and both motionless alike;
> Such is the shelter that is there, and such
> The safeguard for repose and quietness.
>
> Our steeds remounted, and the summons given,
> With whip and spur we by the Chauntry flew
> In uncouth race, and left the cross-legged Knight,
> And the stone-abbot, and that single wren
> Which one day sang so sweetly in the nave
> Of the old church, that, though from recent showers
> The earth was comfortless, and, touch'd by faint
> Internal breezes–sobbings of the place,
> And respirations, from the roofless walls
> The shuddering ivy dripped large drops, yet still,
> So sweetly 'mid the
> gloom the invisible Bird
> Sang to itself that there I
> could have made
> My dwelling-place, and
> lived for ever there
> To hear such music.

Illustration of a grand dinner for 300 guests, held in a giant marquee at the abbey, to celebrate the opening of the Ulverston and Lancaster Railway in 1857

However, by far the greatest stimulus to tourism was the construction of the Furness railway, and a station and hotel right next to the abbey. The line opened in 1847 on a small scale at first, but was expanded to link up with Ulverston and Lancaster ten years later. The Cavendishes sold the manor house to the railway company, and during the 1850s and '60s the building was substantially remodelled to become the Furness Abbey Hotel.

The arrival of the railway did not win universal approval! Wordsworth, in a letter of 1845, wrote, 'What do you think of a Railway being driven as it now is, close to the magnificent memorial of the piety of our ancestors? Many of the trees which embowered the ruin have been felled to make way for this pestilential nuisance.' Thirty years later John Ruskin ironically noted '. . . that glorious England of the future; in which there will be no abbeys (all having been shaken down, as my own sweet Furness is fast being, by the luggage trains)'.

The construction of the railway coincided with the first antiquarian excavations on the site. Thomas Beck directed some clearing of the church in about 1840 when he was researching his book *Annales Furnesienses*, published in 1844. Beck described the rubble inside the west tower as being '. . . so compact by its fall, so tenacious by the rains, and . . . composed of such strongly cemented materials, as to require blasting with gunpowder into manageable pieces for its removal'.

From 1845 the first in a succession of guidebooks to the site was produced. Also at this time the abbey made its appearance in specialist works on Cistercian architecture, most notably those of the Lancaster-based architect and medievalist Edmund Sharpe. The site became a popular subject for the early photographers: both Roger Fenton and Francis Frith worked here. And with the serious study of Gothic architecture, the first accurate drawings and student sketchbooks began to appear.

The early 1880s saw further clearance and the first attempts at devegetation, cleaning and restoration. Some of the claustral buildings were excavated and the walls freed of ivy under W B Kendall's supervision, with the encouragement of Lord Frederick Cavendish.

Above: An early photograph of the north transept taken by Roger Fenton in about 1856 and below, the same view taken several years later showing the extent of repairs and devegetation. Note that the buttress has disappeared

ROYAL PHOTOGRAPHIC SOCIETY

The turn of the century saw the expansion of the Furness Abbey Hotel and enlargement of the station. The abbey now offered conference accommodation as well as an

The Furness Abbey Hotel and station

Sir William St John Hope
Below: The United
Association of Bakers and
Confectioners conference at
the abbey in about 1910

attractive day out for people of the northern industrial towns, despite the hotel's spurious claim to be in the centre of Lakeland! This period also saw the first systematic excavations and archaeological assessment of the site as a whole, under the direction of Sir William St John Hope.

In 1923, Lord Richard Cavendish placed the ruins in the guardianship of the state. The then Office of Works, under Sir Charles Peers, Chief Inspector of Ancient Monuments, immediately set in motion a major programme of restoration. This work was accompanied by a general 'tidying up' of the site, involving burial of fallen architectural fragments, removal of some post-monastic features and further excavations, so that more of the abbey buildings were uncovered and displayed. The abbey's care and continued maintenance have been the responsibility of various government departments since that time.

Except for part of its north wing, the hotel was demolished in 1953, following bomb damage in 1941. Its site is now occupied by the present car park and museum, opened in 1982.

PIEL CASTLE

PIEL CASTLE stands on the south-eastern point of an islet (Piel island) at the mouth of the deep-water harbour at Barrow, guarding the passage to and from the Abbey's holdings in Ireland and the Isle of Man. According to a government report at the time of the Spanish Armada (1588), this was considered the best harbour between Milford Haven in south-west Wales and the Scottish border. Despite the survival of Furness Abbey's chartulary, however, and the imposing nature of the castle ruins, which are visible from all around Morecambe Bay, remarkably little is known of the history and purpose of this monument.

The Abbot and convent were granted a licence to crenellate 'their dwelling-house' in 1327 by Edward III, which suggests the fortification of an existing building. The licence dates from a period when frequent Scottish raids resulted in the construction of many defended houses throughout the Borders.

In 1403, Abbot John de Bolton was accused of lack of maintenance, and the castle was seized into the king's hands, though it was returned in 1411. In 1487 Piel was witness to an event of national importance, when the expedition from Ireland which intended to depose Henry VII in favour of Lambert Simnel, landed here.

Offshore view of Piel Castle and other island buildings

The solid shape of the castle from the south

By 1537, when Furness Abbey was dissolved, the castle was reported to be badly decayed. It was in too ruinous a state to be of any reported strategic value during the Civil Wars, despite the nearby presence of Parliamentary and Royalist forces. From the eighteenth century onwards its gradual ruination can be charted by prints, such as those of the Buck brothers (1727) and Hearne in 1781. It is clear that the island itself was also eroding, exacerbating the decay of the monument, and in the 1850s and 1860s the Duke of Buccleuch undertook the construction of sea defences around the southern and eastern sides which slowed the pace of erosion. Subsequently, in 1876-8, many of the buildings were consolidated. The island was given to Barrow Corporation in 1918, and the castle taken into state guardianship in 1919.

DESCRIPTION

Piel Castle stands on a low mound of boulder clay at the highest point of the island and consists of a keep, with inner and outer baileys each surrounded by a ditch and with towers at the north-eastern, north-western and south-western corners. It is irregular in plan: the large outer bailey only ever existed on the north and west sides. All the structures are of stone taken from the beach, roughly worked and coursed. Architectural detail is of red sandstone, presumably from the quarries surrounding Furness Abbey.

The best approach is from the north, towards the north-eastern corner of the outer bailey. Here, a narrow path leads below the ruinous outer tower which stands on a mound of upcast from the ditch. The path follows a causeway between the ditch and the sea, and traces of stone revetting are visible. This tower is more ornate than the others in the outer bailey, and may once have formed part of the original outer gate: there is no other evidence for a gate through the outer perimeter. Immediately beyond it, a low structure has been traditionally interpreted as the castle's chapel, although its position and style of construction suggest that it was not part of the original plan and may even post-date the formal occupation of the monument. The outer north-western and south-western towers now stand in isolation, and the curtain walls linking them may never have been constructed fully. These towers are of simple construction, each of two storeys, the upper accessed from the curtain wall.

The southern and eastern curtain walls have collapsed onto the beach, and some traces are visible, particularly to the south. It is clear these linked the outer towers with their inner couterparts, which are also now largely collapsed. Access to the inner bailey was through a gatehouse in the western wall, a drawbridge once spanning the ditch. The inner bailey is much smaller than the outer and is dominated by the large three-storey keep, unusually one of three parallel compartments. Access from the gatehouse to the entrance to the keep in its northern wall is cramped, and has resulted in the unusual pentagonal shape of the small north-western tower.

The keep is entered through an attached two-storey gatehouse at first floor level, into the central compartment, although the original entrance was probably into the ground floor. A worn grotesque can still be seen above this, traditionally interpreted as Salome. Much of the eastern compartment collapsed in the early nineteenth century, its remains still lying on the beach. The ground floor was probably of little importance, the main chambers being on the upper floors, particularly in the eastern and western compartments.

The central compartment would have been relatively dark, only naturally lit by large windows in the south wall, a fact recognised by the insertion of internal openings to bring borrowed light into the rooms. A tower at the south-eastern corner may have contained private apartments.

The keep demonstrates features which would deny defence as the primary purpose of Piel Castle. Despite the defensive layout of the monument as a whole, the large windows in its upper floors would make attack easy if the outer defences were breached, perhaps the reason why many first floor windows were blocked in antiquity. It seems likely that the castle as originally conceived may have been designed as a retreat for the Abbot, with the emphasis on domestic comforts, but was subsequently converted to a more utilitarian purpose, probably a customs post to control the Abbey's shipping interests.

Engraving of Piel Castle from 1772 by Samuel and Nathaniel Buck

FURTHER READING AND ❖ ❖ ACKNOWLEDGEMENTS

Beck, T A, 1844, *Annales Furnesienses, History and Antiquities of the Abbey of Furness,* London

Brakspear, H, 1900, The first church at Furness, *Transactions of the Lancashire and Cheshire Antiquarian Society,* vol 18, 70-87

Burton, J, and Kerr, J, 2011, *The Cistercians in the Middle Ages,* Woodbridge

Fielding, T H, and Walton, J, 1821, *A Picturesque Tour of the English Lakes,* London

Fishwick, H (ed), 1899, Pleadings and Depositions in the Duchy Court of Lancaster in the time of Edward VI and Philip and Mary, The Record Society, Lancashire and Cheshire, 40

Gilpin, W, 1786, *Observations relative chiefly to Picturesque Beauty, made in the year 1772, on several parts of England, particularly the Mountains and Lakes of Cumberland and Westmoreland,* London

Green, W, 1819, *The Tourist's New Guide containing a description of the Lakes, Mountains and Scenery in Cumberland, Westmorland and Lancashire,* 2 vols, Kendal

Haigh, C, 1969, *The Last Days of the Lancashire Monasteries and the Pilgrimage of Grace,* Chethan Society, 3rd Series, 17, Manchester

Hearne, T, and Byrne, W, 1786, *Antiquities of Great Britain, illustrated in views of monasteries, castles and churches now existing,* London

Hope, 1900, The Abbey of St Mary in Furness, Lancashire, *Transactions of the Cumberland and Westmorland Antiquarian and Archaeological Society,* os16, 221-302

Housman, J, 1816, *A Descriptive Tour and Guide to the Lakes, Caves, Mountains and other Natural Curiosities in Cumberland, Westmorland, Lancashire and a part of the West Riding of Yorkshire,* 7th edition, Carlisle

Radcliffe, A, 1795, *A Journey made in the summer of 1794 through Holland and the Western frontier of Germany with a return down the Rhine, to which are added observations during a tour of the Lakes of Lancashire, Westmorland and Cumberland,* London

Robinson, D (ed), 1998, *The Cistercian Abbeys of Britain: Far from the Concourse of Men,* London

Swarbrick, J, 1929, *The Reparation of Furness Abbey,* National Ancient Monuments Review, 2, 5, 204-8; 6, 263-70.

Vetusta Monumenta I, 1747, Society of Antiquaries of London

West, T, 1774, *Antiquities of Furness: or an account of the Royal Abbey of St Mary...,* London [revised edition by W Close, Ulverston (1805)]

Whitaker, T, 1823, *An History of Richmondshire in the North Riding of the County of York; together with those parts of the everwicschire of Domesday which form the Wapentakes of Lonsdale, Ewecross and Amunderness in the Counties of York, Lancaster and Westmorland,* 2 vols, London

Wilkinson, J, 1810, *Select Views in Cumberland, Westmorland and Lancashire,* London

Wood, J, 1992, Furness Abbey: An integrated and multi-disciplinary approach to the survey, recording, analysis and interpretation of a monastic building, in *Medieval Europe 1992, Volume 6: Religion and Belief,* York, 163-70.

Wood, J, 2008, *Visualizations of Furness Abbey: from romantic ruin to computer model,* English Heritage Historical Review, 3, 8-35.

Jason Wood is grateful for the assistance of Geoffry and Janet Martin for comments on historical material, and Michael Wheeler and Gill Chitty for advice on the selection of literary sources.